Also in this series:

LIFE'S LITTLE INSTRUCTION BOOK
LIFE'S LITTLE INSTRUCTION BOOK VOL II
THE LOVERS' LITTLE INSTRUCTION BOOK
THE DOG'S LITTLE INSTRUCTION BOOK
THE CAT'S LITTLE INSTRUCTION BOOK

THE PARENTS'
LITTLE INSTRUCTION
BOOK

Cindy Francis

Thorsons
An Imprint of HarperCollins*Publishers*

Thorsons
An Imprint of HarperCollins Publishers
77–85 Fulham Palace Road
Hammersmith, London W6 8JB

First published in the USA by Newport House, Inc.,
107 R. R. 620 S., Suite 7-A, Austin, TX 78734
Thorsons edition 1994
1 3 5 7 9 10 8 6 4 2

© Cindy Francis 1993

Cindy Francis asserts the moral right
to be identified as the author of this work

A catalogue record for this book is available
from the British Library

ISBN 0 7225 3101 X

Printed in Great Britain by
HarperCollinsManufacturing Glasgow

To My Mother,
Donna Kress

Introduction

Years ago, when I was expecting my first child, I had many long talks with my mother about what she had learned while bringing up me and my five brothers and sisters. She had done a wonderful job, while having a lot more fun than other mothers I knew. What, I wondered, were her secrets? My mother and I would talk and talk, and after she would go, I'd write down the lessons I had learned.

As a parent, I followed these simple lessons and added my own, and I've been greatly rewarded for having them to guide and inspire me. The 'terrible twos' were for me 'terrific twos' and all the years since have been the richest of my life.

Following the publication of my previous book *The Lover's Little Instruction Book* many of you wrote to ask me to put together a book for mothers. I was delighted, and called the most successful and happy mothers I know to ask if they had any lessons to add. I've also looked through lots of books by 'experts', and found that the gist of what they had to say could usually be put in a sentence or two. The UK publishers, Thorsons, decided to call this book The Parents' Little Instruction Book as so many of today's fathers are taking such an active role in the upbringing of their children.

I'm excited and pleased to present you now with my little instructions for parents. I hope you'll not only read and enjoy them, but will take them to heart and live them.

The greatest gift you have to give your children is you.

When you talk to your child, mostly listen.

Take care of yourself, so you can take care of others.

Change is inevitable, so welcome it.

Always give in to the urge to hug your child.

Setting limits is good for children. They'll complain, but what they'll feel is relief.

🐭 You'll never be an 'Absolutely Perfect Parent'. Be a 'Good Enough Parent'.

🐭 If things don't work out, it's okay to cry– but also learn.

Teach your children they're unique. That way, they won't feel pressure to be like everybody else.

 Ask your child what she likes most to do with you. Do that more often.

Say 'I'm sorry' when you're wrong.

Your child will do as you do, not as you say. So set a good example.

Catch your child doing things right.

Be loving, even when you don't feel loving.

Forgive yourself for the mistakes you have made.

Encourage your child every chance you get.

Be flexible with rules.

🐾 Recognize and accept your child's feelings.

🐾 Look for win/win solutions.

🐾 Remember that when you tell your child to act their age, they probably already are.

Some time each day, give your child your undivided attention.

Ask for your child's opinion more often.

If you feel overwhelmed, just start doing one thing at a time.

Tell your children, 'I love you just the way you are'.

Take time out every day to have fun.

Give your children opportunities to make real contributions to the family.

Go to the park. Everybody plays!

 Don't compare your children to others. Value them each for their own gifts.

Little instructions you can learn from your children:

Play more.

Be curious.

Get all wrapped up in what you're doing.

Even the littlest things can bring you pleasure.

Treat your children the way you wish you had been treated when you were a youngster.

Show your respect by introducing your child by name to everyone who comes over.

Be your child's biggest fan.

Tell your child, 'My life is so much better because you are here'.

 When your child is angry, say out loud, 'I think you need a big hug' – and then give it!

Having your house look like House Beautiful isn't a good use of time. Settle for House Pretty Clean.

 Get up early and watch the sunrise together.

 Exercise together.

Build an extended family, whether it's made up of relatives or friends.

 Plant a tree together.

 When there's conflict, focus on the role you play.

To belong is your children's underlying goal—even when they're misbehaving. Give them constructive ways to belong.

 Go to a procession.

 Spend time together in the library.

Ask questions that begin with 'How,' 'Why,' and 'Tell me about.' These encourage children to speak up.

Build your children's self-esteem by letting them solve most of their own problems.

Have a special time each week for you
and your child to do something together.
With a teenager, ask for this time
because you need it.

 Go to a pond and skip stones.

Children will believe what you say. So be sure what you say builds them up.

Do what you feel is right for your children, regardless of what –'everyone else is doing.'

Teach that what other kids say about them is just their opinion, not the truth.

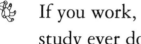 If you work, don't feel guilty. Every single study ever done shows children of working mothers do just as well as other children.

 Be grateful for your family—problems and all.

 Have more family picnics.

Go bird watching together.

Nothing happens by itself. You have to work at having a good family life.

Let your children have their own books.

Give up comparing your family with the Brady Bunch/The Waltons images you grew up with. Those were TV fantasies; your family is real.

 Bake biscuits together from scratch.

Take time to be apart from your children. It will give you all a chance to grow.

 Given a little training and a little practice, most children can far exceed our expectations.

 Toast the sunset with a glass of juice.

Children misbehave when they feel useless. Let them help with cooking, gardening, record-keeping. And when they're older, help them find jobs.

 Praise your child for sharing.

Keep your perspective. Problems ' come to pass' – not to stay.

Meet your children's friends. Meet their parents too, and keep in touch with them so you can compare notes.

Compliment more than you criticise.

Teach your children good eating habits when they're young and they'll keep them all their lives.

 Have family projects like putting up a birdhouse, planting a garden and starting a family album.

Encouragements kids would benefit from
hearing more often:

'Thanks! You really made a difference.'

'I couldn't have done it better myself.'

'I enjoyed working on that with you.'

'You've improved!'

'I have faith in you.'

Even if your child isn't good at listening to you, she will certainly be good at imitating you.

Give your children problems like, 'How can we cut our electricity bill?' Let them research answers and help with solutions.

Send your children on a first aid course.

Let your children know they can always express themselves freely to you about anything.

 Take a nature ramble together.

 Have your own outside interests. Don't live through your children.

Teach your children your family's history, the struggles and successes that led to all of you being where you are.

Talk about values if you expect your child to grow up with values.

Most things that can go wrong, don't.

 When things do go wrong, keep your perspective in describing them. Most aren't 'terrible,' just 'unfortunate'.

🐾 Keep your promises.

🐾 Everybody help recycle newspapers.

🐾 Help your child become an expert at something, whether it's playing the flute, ballet, karate, or gladiator cards.

You'll never get everyone's approval of everything you do as a parent. So don't bother trying.

 Tell your children how proud you are of them.

Let your children know that if there's trouble, you'll always be there.

 Invite over positive people who feel good about themselves.

Let your children 'overhear' you praising them.

 Look for the evening star together. Make a wish.

🐭 Make sure your child understands new rules. Do this by asking her to tell you the rule in her own words.

🐭 Have Polynesia night, with everyone dressed like natives.

Hear your children out, even if you think your answer will be no.

 Make it clear your love doesn't depend on their performance.

Talk about the lessons to be learned from other people's mistakes.

 Everyone—not just you—can help out around the house.

Read Gael Lindenfield's *Confident Children* to learn better ways to raise responsible children.

 Make it clear you like compliments, too. When you do a good job, say, 'Okay, I'm open for compliments!'

It's easy for mothers to become isolated. Spend time with friends. And if you don't have them, make them.

When you need help, ask for it.

Have a family movie night, complete with pizza and popcorn.

 Be firm where safety is concerned.

If your child has problems with school work, get help right away, before he gets really behind.

Put on old records and twist with your child.

To relate better, sit or kneel down to your child's level.

 If your child has an overcrowded schedule, help him cut out something.

If your child wants to talk or play when you're busy, set a time and promise him attention then.

Although you have a powerful connection, your child is separate and has different needs, emotions, and desires. Respect them.

Go bike riding together.

If you've got questions about your child's behaviour, ask other parents.

If you've got serious questions, see a paediatrician or counsellor. Ask for help for both your child and you.

🐭 Work on problems while they're small.

🐭 Share with your child your own life lessons.

🐭 Read 'Feelings' together.

🐻 Balance is the key. Balance work with play, time with the children with time alone.

🐻 When you listen, focus on what your child is feeling.

Be sure your child gets familiar with computers.

 You are not responsible for everything going well for everyone all the time.

Ask your children questions about things they are interested in.

For one day, count how many times you criticize—and praise—your children. Work at criticizing less and praising more.

Talk problems out.

 When you're working around the house, explain what you're doing and ask for help.

 Plan family activities, so watching TV isn't the only thing to do.

🧸 Show your children you're on their side.

🧸 Pause, and take stock of what really matters to you. Put your time and energy there.

🧸 Quality time is important, but sometimes so is the quantity of time.

Visualize success for yourself and your children.

 Give your children some privacy.

Tell your child what to do instead of what not to do.

Take a warm bubble bath after the kids are in bed.

As your children grow older the way you treat them needs to keep pace. Much teenage rebellion comes from treating them like they're 10 when they're 15.

Everyone in the family name three things every other person does well.

 Read Ray Josephs' *How to Gain an Extra Hour Every Day* to get organized.

Give your full attention when you talk. Don't read or watch TV.

 Teach your children there are better ways than whining and hitting to solve problems.

Instead of ordering your kids to put on sweaters and jackets, let them carry them and put them on if they feel cold.

 Tell your children how special they are to you.

Make having fun a priority!

 To produce a happy child, be a happy parent.

 Every weekend, explore together somewhere new in your area.

Get involved in your child's education by working positively with the school.

 Read *Calvin and Hobbes* together. Ask why the characters act the funny way they do.

Blow up a balloon and play volleyball with it.

 Important lesson: life isn't fair.

You can teach your children how to clean their rooms, but don't expect too much.

 Punish your children by withdrawing privileges.

Solve a puzzle together.

 It takes two to make an argument. Don't be one of them.

Nurture your child—not just with food, but with kind words as well.

 Get together with other mothers and fathers and swap stories.

Start a journal to keep track of what you've learned and the successes you've had.

 Get a book on parenting and look up what to expect at your child's age.

Have lighthearted 'punishments':
Whoever has her elbows on the table
must sing a song.
Swear words = 10p
Saying something negative about another
family member = 25p

Enjoy the gifts life is presenting you at this moment.

 Never criticize in front of others.

When you're upset, be careful not to say things you might regret.

 Take lots of pictures.

 Sometimes, when your children expect punishment, give them a big hug instead.

For a laugh, read together Hawkins' *Monsters* and *Pirates books,* and for very young children try *Cat in Hat* and anything else by Dr Seuss.

Show your love by being kind.

Growth comes with frustration.
Be a source of support.

Once you have criticized your child's
actions, don't bring it up again.

Tell your child often, 'I love you, no matter what.'

 Set reasonable limits.

At bedtime, establish a routine that winds thing down and get your child ready for sleep.

Have fruit and vegetables–instead of sweets–for your kids to snack on.

Think how you'd feel in your child's place.

Have a special dinner in honour of your children.

Share memories of when you were your child's age.

 When your child gets discouraged, remind her of all the things she couldn't do not long ago—and now can.

At night, sit outside on a blanket and look at the stars.

 Hold family meetings to clear up gripes.

Set up a tent in the living room and have dinner in it.

Treat all your children equally.

Have your kids take music lessons. Let them stop if they don't like it.

 Rituals, like having dinner together, make children feel more secure.

How to communicate when you and your child are mad: One person talks at a time. The listener has to give back the gist of what the talker says to the talker's satisfaction before she gets her turn to speak.

Arguing Do's:

Bring up one problem at a time.
Focus on the problem.
Be specific about your complaints.
Compromise if possible.

Arguing Don'ts:

No yelling or swearing.
No name-calling.
No questioning motives.
No bringing up the past.

Even if your child fails, praise the effort.

Praise–not just success–but also improvement.

Lie on the floor and read the encyclopedia together.

Your children provide you with a second chance to do the things you loved as a youngster.
Take that chance.

Cook a meal together, with everybody in charge of one dish.

 If you're too busy to have fun with your children, you're too busy.

When you're driving, hand your child a map and ask her to direct you to your destination.

Compliment your children often, and you'll give them a reputation to live up to!

Sing songs around a campfire.

Let your children progress at their own speed.

If the discipline you're using isn't working, do something different.

The behaviour may be bad, but never the child.

If you expect your children to be 'perfect,' you will always be disappointed.

See who can make the funniest face.

 Teach that failure is never final unless you give up.

Once a month, spend a whole day doing whatever your child wants to do.

Be happy as your children need you less and less. That's how it's supposed to be.

Teach that while the 'easy way' in the short run is to be lazy and mess about in school, that often turns out to be the hard way in the long run.

Three steps to take when children misbehave:

1. Briefly describe the behaviour.
2. Tell how you feel about it.
3. Affirm that you know the child can do better.

Pause, and notice the beauty around you.

Instead of coaxing your children out of bed every morning, buy them alarm clocks. If they're late, let them have the consequences.

Stay out of your children's fights unless someone is in danger. Let them work things out themselves.

 Surprise your child with little gifts.

The best way to get your children to listen to you is to listen to them.

 Let family privileges coincide with responsibilities.

Never say your child is 'shy.' Instead, explain, 'She doesn't want to talk right now.'

 If your child acts shy, practise with her in front of a mirror smiling, making eye contact, and keeping her legs and arms uncrossed.

🐾 Tell your children stories in which they are the heroes.

🐾 When your kids grow up, they won't remember if the house was perfectly neat and clean. But they will remember whether or not you spent time with them.

Better to be a model than a critic.

 When you get angry, remember it's the result of your thinking, not what your child is doing.

Teach that no one is perfect—not you, not them, not anyone. And nothing is perfect. But it's possible to be happy in an imperfect world.

When your child tells you problems, show you really understand by repeating the essence of what you heard and asking if you're right.

 When you're excited, let it show!

Have talks at bedtime. Your child will talk more in order to stay up later.

Fly a kite together.

Send your children off in the morning with a hug.

A positive word or smile every day can propel your child to success.

 Replenish yourself by taking time to be alone.

 Help a charity together.

The only person you can control is yourself.

 Build trust by going on a 'blind walk,' in which you take turns closing your eyes and being led around.

 Encourage your child to think BIG!

Teach your children the immediate bad consequences of smoking—it makes you cough and your breath and clothes smell bad. Children seldom think long-term.

Teach also the immediate bad consequences of drinking—it makes it hard for you to think and learn and play. It makes you say and do stupid things you may regret later. And it often makes you have bad accidents.

Everyone tape a message to send to someone far away.

 Don't do for children what they can do for themselves.

 When your children outgrow their clothes, give the clothes to the poor.

For one day, keep track of all the sugar your child eats. Put that amount in a bottle and show it to her.

Report cards are your child's—not yours.

Let your children see that you have shortcomings and suffer setbacks. This will help them be more realistic about themselves.

 Nurture yourself, too.

Go to car boot sales together.

Help your child plan short-term goals (like going camping) and long-term goal (like going to college).

Let your child have input into solutions for problems, especially those which concern her.

If you can afford it, get help with your housework.

Try to have a sit-down family meal at least three times a week. Turn off all distractions like the TV and stereo.

🧸 When your child takes a wrong turn, gently help her get back on track.

🧸 Keep instructions simple.

🧸 Play with your child every day.

Plan your child's parties around activities like swimming and bowling.

 Be consistent.

 Attend your child's school activities.

🐾 Mark off your child's height on a closet wall. Watch them grow!

🐾 You can't assume your kids understand their homework. Look it over to see if they need help.

🐾 Solve puzzles together.

Put a surprise note under everybody's plate at dinner.

 When you're angry, take five minutes to cool off.

 Kids sometimes have to make their own mistakes before they learn from them.

At bedtime, get the conversation going by asking, 'What's the best thing that happened to you today? The worst?'

Use the past tense when criticizing. For example, say 'you forgot' rather than 'you always forget.'

Let your child take responsibility for her actions–and for coping with what follows.

 Read your children stories about successful people.

 Be specific with praise. It'll mean more.

Make a list of everything you have to do each day. Do the most important first.

Shower your kids with kindness!

Be honest (they'll know if you're not anyway).

Have "Family Night" once a week. Everybody does something fun together.

 Follow the rules yourself that you set for your child.

 Have a family Ping-Pong contest!

Read Nick Butterworth's *Percy Park* books with your child.

If you work, take your child with you so she'll understand what it is you do.

Give gifts that encourage fitness, such as skates and bikes.

Substitute low-fat frozen yogurt for ice cream; crackers for chocolate chip biscuits; mixed nuts for crisps.

 Always be on the lookout for something positive to say.